Delphiniums

Civic Garden Centre Library

D0107795

Cover: a promising seedling from delphinium 'Cassius', raised by the author
Overleaf: the spectacular new University Hybrid red delphiniums
(both photographs by David Bassett)

Delphiniums

A Wisley handbook

David Bassett

 Cassell

The Royal Horticultural Society

Cassell Educational Limited
Artillery House, Artillery Row
London SW1P 1RT
for the Royal Horticultural Society

First published 1990

British Library Cataloguing in Publication Data

Bassett, David
  Delphiniums.
  1. Gardens. Delphiniums
  I. Title   II. Royal Horticultural Society
  III. Series
  635.9′33111

  ISBN 0-304-31812-4

Photographs by David Bassett and Michael Warren
Line drawings by David Bassett
Design by Lesley Stewart
Phototypesetting by Chapterhouse Ltd, Formby
Printed in Hong Kong by Wing King Tong Co. Ltd

Contents

Delphiniums add distinction to a herbaceous border

Introduction

The range of colours in the flowers of hardy plants covers the complete spectrum. However, while for reds, pinks, yellows and whites there are many plants of differing shapes and sizes, for clear blues the choice is more limited. Asked to name some blue flowers, we might think of forget-me-nots or gentians and a few others, but the most popular choice would probably be delphiniums. These plants seem to have a special place in our affections and they amply repay our attentions, responding to good cultivation with spectacular blooms that few other garden flowers can match. The best delphiniums available today are the result of careful selection and skilful hybridization, carried out by a small number of dedicated amateur and professional growers in several countries, notably Frank Reinelt, the raiser in the USA of the Giant Pacific Strain, and Frank Bishop and the Langdons in Britain. The peak of their activities was the first half of the twentieth century, but the qualities they introduced live on and continue to be exploited. Plant breeders are still seeking new delphiniums in colours and sizes to match the ever-changing fashions of the market. Recent years have seen a greater emphasis on shorter growth and the introduction of new colours in the brilliant reds and clear pinks of the University Hybrids.

This handbook describes the basic requirements for growing delphiniums and explores the scope for making use in our gardens of the wide range of colours and plant forms available. The cultivation methods recommended are ones that I have found successful in growing my own delphiniums, initially in a small garden and latterly on a larger scale. When I began about 25 years ago, I followed the approach outlined by Ronald Parrett in his Penguin Handbook. Since that time, I have tried many other ways of doing things, often as a result of articles by Tom Cowan, Colin Edwards and others in the Year Books of the Delphinium Society. Methods that were more successful and reliable than the old ones became my standard practice and are included here. This is true, for example, of the technique of rooting cuttings in a jar of water, which allows any gardener to increase stock of these lovely plants, no matter what facilities are available. Hopefully, this book will encourage others to experiment a little, to grow a few more delphiniums and to share the pleasure I get from their beautiful flowers.

Delphiniums in the wild and in cultivation

Several distinct types of delphinium are widely cultivated as garden plants. There are annuals grown from seed each year, more commonly known as larkspurs; short-growing plants for the rock garden; branching kinds for borders and cutting; and the tall perennial hybrids with magnificent blooms. This range of characteristics is merely a selection from those of the 250 or more delphinium species, which grow in the wild in many parts of the northern hemisphere. Most delphinium species are probably of little value in the garden, but it is interesting to look at some that illustrate general attributes of the plants and their potential for the introduction of new characters into garden delphiniums.

The first feature of a flowering plant to attract us is its flowers. With any delphinium, the most distinctive characteristic is the spur projecting backwards from the top petal, which contains the nectary that helps attract pollinating insects to the flower, as do the brightly coloured petals. These outer "petals" are really the sepals of a delphinium flower and the true petals form the eye or bee at the centre of the floret. Since gardeners normally call the outer set of coloured sepals petals, that name will be used here and should not lead to any confusion. Species delphiniums usually have just five petals and such flowers are described as being single. Many cultivated hybrids have semi-double or fully double flowers, with multiple sets of petals, eye petals, stamens and seed pods.

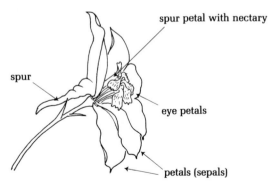

Figure 1: characteristic parts of the floret of a garden hybrid delphinium (some sepals have been removed to show the structure more clearly)

Delphinium flowers differ considerably from one species to another. Some that mostly flower in dry conditions have showy, wide-open flowers, while others from the high Himalaya and tropical Africa hang their heads to protect the pollen. Often the flowers are quite small relative to the size of the plants, being typically $\frac{1}{2}$–1 in. (10–25 mm) across. This is not too important for garden use if the plants flower as prolifically as the European annual species, D. consolida, or the perennials D. grandiflorum and D. tatsienense from China. These produce masses of flowers on short, branched stems and are widely cultivated. D. requieni, an easily grown biennial from Corsica, also has many tiny florets, which individually have the charm of a miniature orchid and are arranged in an impressive bloom spike and in long sprays developing from the leaf axils (see p. 10). Incorporating the flower size and colours of garden larkspurs into this species would perhaps yield novel delphiniums of considerable splendour.

A fascinating feature of wild delphiniums is the great colour range. The lovely clear blues of D. grandiflorum and D. tatsienense are complemented by pure white forms of these species (see p. 16), which are easy to grow. There are also deep violets and rosy purples in D. hansenii from California (see p. 10). Most spectacular, however, are the bright scarlet of two other Californians, D. cardinale and the dwarf D. nudicaule, and the primrose-yellow of D. zalil from Iran (see pp. 12 and 10). East Africa provides two gems in D. macrocentrum, with curious, greeny blue flowers more like those of a cottage-garden aquilegia, and D. leroyi, with its deliciously fragrant, white flowers.

The species mentioned grow in a wide range of habitats where they experience extremes of temperature or summer drought. Their foliage and root systems are well adapted to those environments and vary substantially between species. Many annual and biennial species are moderately hardy and seedlings germinating in autumn can survive winter frost as green plants. Their flower stems lengthen when spring growth starts and may be either slender and hard, as in D. consolida, or fleshy and hollow, like the thick stems of D. requieni. These species do not make a permanent rootstock and die after setting seed. Perennial delphinium species show similiar variations in stem and leaf form with some, for example D. zalil, having slim stems and highly dissected foliage, while others have thick, fleshy stems and large leaves. The crucial difference is in the rootstock, which in all perennial species develops as a tough woody "crown" (sometimes like a tuber) that lives for many years. The flowering stems grow out in spring from crown buds or eyes, which are formed at flowering time the previous year and then remain dormant through periods of

Above (left): a species delphinium from the mountains in Colorado, USA; (right) *D. requieni*, a biennial species from Corsica, with woolly stems

Below (left): *D. hansenii*, a Californian species, has impressively dark flowers; (right) *D. zalil*, a tuberous-rooted perennial from Iran, needs careful cultivation

drought in summer or autumn and through the cold of severe winters. In the dormant state, the rootstock of most perennial species is extremely hardy and can withstand prolonged severe frost.

The special adaptations of delphinium species to alpine or desert conditions can make them difficult to please in the generally mild and damp winters of Britain. Even for cultivated delphiniums, the weather is seldom sufficiently cold to force plants into the extended period of dormancy that would be normal for alpine species like *D. elatum*, from which our garden hybrids are derived. Often the plants make early growth that is quite susceptible to frost damage, and mild winters may lead to more losses than exceptionally cold years.

The best selections of cultivated delphiniums differ in many ways from the species. The work of plant breeders in cross-breeding one species with another and in repeatedly selecting seedlings over many generations has produced plants with greatly improved characteristics for garden decoration. The cultivated hybrids typically have larger flowers with more petals than the wild flowers and carry more flowers on each stem. In recent years, growers have selected for other characters, such as short growth and conical bloom spikes.

The improvements obtained by hybridization and selection are clearly seen in named cultivars of the perennial hybrids derived from *D. elatum*. For example, in blooms of 'Emily Hawkins', the individual florets are nearly 3 in. (7 cm) in diameter, with 13 pale violet petals of flat, rounded shape and a neat cluster of light brown, contrasting eye petals (see pp. 12 and 58). These florets are packed in a beautifully regular manner, without overcrowding or ugly gaps, to form a tapering spike of colour about 3 ft (90 cm) long. The flowers open right to the top of the bloom before petals start to drop at the base, as opposed to the rapid shedding of petals so characteristic of single-flowered types. The colour range for the cultivars is also wider than for *D. elatum* itself and includes pure whites, pale greyish lavenders or mauve-pinks, creamy whites with yellow eyes, a huge number of blues and mauve of every shade, dusky pinks, royal purples and deep violets.

The emphasis in the breeding of perennial hybrids by both amateurs and commercial growers in Britain has been on the selection of elite individual plants, like 'Emily Hawkins', for introduction to commerce as named cultivars. Such plants do not breed true from seed, but must be propagated from cuttings and, although named cultivars are available from specialists, their sales no longer support costly breeding programmes. However, new named cultivars continue to come from amateur raisers and

11

Left: 'Emily Hawkins', a first-class named cultivar of the popular perennial hybrid delphiniums
Right: *D. cardinale*, the scarlet larkspur of southern California, is best raised from seed to flower the same year

a visit to the delphinium trials at the Royal Horticultural Society's Garden, Wisley, shows that high standards are being maintained.

Growing conditions in many areas of the United States are less favourable for long-lived perennial delphiniums and the emphasis there has been on producing selections that will come true to colour from seed. The Giant Pacific Strain raised by Frank Reinelt in California combined superb quality of bloom with reliable reproduction of the colour in individual selections, from the whites of the 'Galahad' and 'Percival' series and blues of 'Summer Skies', to the intense purples of 'King Arthur' and the dusky pinks of the 'Astolat' and 'Elaine' series. Plants raised from seed derived from the Pacific Giants are probably the most readily available delphiniums in commerce.

Other types of delphinium have been improved in similar ways. For example, hybridization and selection for branching growth

Opposite: the magnificent blue delphinium, 'Loch Nevis'

resulted in the attractive cultivars known as Belladonnas, which produce clear blue or white single flowers over a long period. The annual larkspurs also differ substantially from wild forms, having double flowers, more compact bloom spikes than their wild ancestors and a wide colour range. The blues are poor, but there are good purples, clear whites, and pink shades from salmon to carmine that are superior to any of the dusky pinks found in *elatum* hybrids. However, these pinks and reds still do not have the brilliance of the red flowers of *D. cardinale* and this presents plant breeders with a great challenge.

D. cardinale, a tuberous-rooted perennial with a very rangy growth habit, is not well suited for garden cultivation in Britain, but several hybridists have tried to combine its colour with the growth habit of other cultivated delphiniums. Most recently, Dr R. A. Legro, working at Wageningen University in Holland and latterly at the RHS Garden, Wisley, has developed the University Hybrids, which produce flowers in a wide range of sharp pinks, brilliant reds and apricot-orange. After more than 25 years of painstaking work, involving crosses between the red species and the normal garden cultivars and selection of the best plants through many generations of crosses between seedlings, these spectacular plants should soon be setting our gardens alight (see pp. 2 and 64).

The introduction of true red and pink perennial delphiniums seems assured, but there remain many other objectives for plant breeders. With the techniques of genetic engineering now available, there is no reason why we should not dream of delphiniums with flowers of buttercup-yellow or with the sweet scent of *D. leroyi*. However, a quick look around gardens shows that all such novelties are as fragile as the beauty of the flowers themselves. The reality is that most delphiniums grown differ little from the wild flowers. The characteristics we count as "improvements" are genetically recessive and are quickly lost in subsequent generations, when insect pollination leads to random crossing of the best cultivars with the worst. There is thus an excellent reason for all delphinium-lovers to try their hand at plant selection or hybridization. Many amateur gardeners have done so in the past and have contributed much to the high quality of delphiniums for our gardens.

Using delphiniums in the garden

Although delphiniums are not unduly fussy, the results obtained at flowering time depend significantly on soil and situation and it pays to consider these factors when deciding where to plant them.

The ideal site for all cultivated delphiniums is an open position in full sun, as might be found at the middle of a field. Such conditions produce sturdy plants with a more compact growth habit than is commonly seen in gardens, where surrounding trees, fences, high buildings or too close planting cause the stems and blooms to stretch up to the light. Tall delphiniums are not suitable for growing in heavy shade, although partial shading by trees can be advantageous in reducing bleaching of the paler flower colours in sunny weather. For shaded positions, it is worth experimenting with some of the short-growing and branching types, like the cultivated forms of *D. grandiflorum* and the Belladonnas.

While high light and good air circulation are important for top growth, the soil must provide nutrients and a plentiful supply of water for the roots, without them suffering from waterlogging.

A colourful display of delphiniums in the author's garden

The white form of *D. tatsienense* makes a pretty edging for a bed which also includes the red *D. cardinale*

These requirements are best met by soils with some clay content, which are more water-retentive than hungry sand. However, the structure of most soils can be improved enough to grow good delphiniums, by incorporating compost or manure, and nutrient levels can be raised by adding fertilizer (see p. 21). Soils with a neutral pH are perhaps the ideal, but soil acidity does not seem very significant as excellent delphiniums can be grown on acid sand and on alkaline clays over chalk. Positions close to trees are often associated with unfavourable soil conditions, owing to competition from the tree roots, which make it difficult to maintain sufficiently high levels of nutrients and water in the soil.

Where the soil is very unfavourable or open ground is not available, delphiniums can be grown in containers. The potting compost can then be adjusted to suit the plant, although keeping up with the watering demands of large delphiniums in pots means much extra work, especially in hot weather. This is a particularly good way to handle species delphiniums, for it is then easier to meet special requirements, such as the need for dry soil conditions during the dormant period of species with tuberous roots. Another advantage of container-grown plants is that they can be moved about in the garden and also taken into the greenhouse, to force growth for propagation or early flowering. Quite magnificent blooms can be produced by forcing, as the displays at the Chelsea Flower Show demonstrate.

Delphiniums are particularly good plants for mixed borders, in both large and small gardens. The towering bloom spikes of the tall perennial hybrids are excellent at the back of a border and shorter cultivars are ideal for adding interest and changing levels nearer the front. In a small garden, a single plant may provide sufficient colour, but in a larger border it is better to use groups of plants of matching colours, keeping the groups small so that the gaps are not too obtrusive when the flowers are finished. The Belladonnas, with their more branched flowering habit, are especially useful for providing mounds of blue in the middle of a border. Although they lack the dramatic impact of their taller cousins, they have the advantage of needing less attention to staking. The short-growing hybrids of *D. grandiflorum* are lovely at the front of a border, as are dwarf species like *D. nudicaule*. Winter losses of these types are often high, but replacements are easily raised from seed saved from the previous year (see p. 28).

In choosing delphiniums for borders, it it worth giving some thought to flower colour in relation to the surrounding plants. White delphiniums are particularly dramatic and can be enhanced by a background of dark foliage or by neighbouring plants with flowers in strong colours. Blue delphiniums cause few problems in siting as the strong blues can be used to contrast with other bright colours, while the pastel blues and lavender tinges blend well with the pale violets of campanulas and the flowers of many other border plants. The strong purples of some delphiniums can be quite difficult to match with other flowers, but look marvellous set off by a yellow carpet of *Anthemis tinctoria* flowers hiding the delphinium stems. The dusky pink cultivars can be difficult too, but their effect is greatly heightened by plants with grey or silver foliage. The only limit to what can be achieved in a planting scheme is our own imaginations and, if the result turns out to be unsatisfactory, it can always be changed by moving the plants around.

The best selections of perennial delphiniums are so eye-catching in flower that they can be given a separate island bed, containing anything from one or two plants to a hundred or more. A good position for the bed is immediately behind a herbaceous border, where the blooms add to the show of border flowers (see p. 18). This has the advantage that it is easy to attend to the special needs of the delphiniums without tramping among the other plants. However, a delphinium bed can become a rather unsightly mess after flowering, unless it is interplanted with other plants, such as dahlias and spray chrysanthemums, to continue the flower display through to late autumn.

Despite their alpine origins, many delphiniums are too large for

A separate delphinium bed behind a herbaceous border is easy to maintain and avoids disturbing other plants

the rock garden, but it is here that the dwarf species and the hybrids derived from *D. grandiflorum* are best placed. Small pockets of good soil among boulders make ideal sites for these little plants and their flowers are usually seen to better effect than in perennial borders. It is also easier to ensure the good drainage required for the survival of the woody or tuberous rootstocks through the winter, although slugs and snails can be a problem because of the many hiding places for them among the rocks.

The relatively short flowering period of delphiniums is a disadvantage that is usually overcome by mixing them with other plants. However, there are several ways to obtain flowers throughout the spring and summer. Keeping a few pot-grown plants in a cool greenhouse from early January can yield good flowers in April or May, although it is advisable to use short cultivars as the stems tend to become drawn up under low light conditions. In the garden, the flowering season can be extended to almost ten weeks by growing a mixture of cultivars with different flowering periods. A further extension into the autumn is possible if the plants are induced to flower again by cutting them down to the ground immediately after flowering. A less drastic alternative is to use either seedlings from early sowings, or cuttings rooted in early spring and planted out in May or June (see p. 32). With proper cultivation, these make vigorous growth and each plant will normally produce one good bloom in August or

18

September. Grown like this, delphiniums represent a useful addition to the normal range of summer bedding plants.

Larkspurs can be sown in early spring direct into the open ground where they are to flower and they can be used in bedding schemes or to fill gaps in a border where colour is needed in late July and August. Most larkspurs are quite hardy and will stand through the winter if sown in autumn, when the plants will grow larger and produce more blooms than from spring sowings. Larkspurs are commonly regarded as making better cut flowers than perennial delphiniums, but the flower character and quality of the perennials is so different that the keen flower arranger would be well advised to grow both sorts.

'Olive Poppleton' is one of the earliest perennial hybrids to flower

Cultivation

Perennial delphiniums have a period of dormancy during the winter months and the season really gets under way in early spring as the plants start into growth, pushing the new shoots out of the ground into the light. From that point on, our task is to ensure that the plants have adequate supplies of nutrients and water and to obtain the best possible display of flowers by a few simple operations to control growth and combat pests and diseases. When the flowers are over, the plants need a little more

The vigorous rootstock of a healthy delphinium, showing the permanent crown from which the flowering stems grow up each year

Room can be found for delphiniums even in a small garden

attention to keep their crowns and roots in good condition through the following winter and ready for another year. Given this care, they should live for many years. However, it is easy to insure against the possibility of losses by taking cuttings or by growing some plants from seeds. This provides young plants with the vigorous root systems required for satisfactory results, and their flowers in late summer are a useful bonus.

SOIL PREPARATION, PLANTING AND TRANSPLANTING

The first point to consider in cultivating delphiniums is the soil preparation necessary before planting. The large-flowered cultivars must have very fertile soil to flower well and good drainage to be long-lived. It is therefore worth trying to improve the soil structure and nutrient levels by incorporating well rotted manure or garden compost, especially in heavy clay soils. Ideally, this should be done in autumn or winter, well before the plants are put in but, if that has not been possible, fork a few bucketfuls of friable garden compost into the site for a new plant at planting time. To increase the supply of nutrients, add at the same time a generous dressing of a general fertilizer with a slow-release component. A mixture of blood, fish and bonemeal is particularly suitable or one can use Growmore, applying it at a rate of 4 oz per sq. yd (100 g/m²).

The best time to plant and transplant delphiniums is spring, when the roots are making growth and the plants will quickly become established at their new sites. However, purchased plants are generally available as young rooted cuttings in early summer and can be planted then. If necessary, the plants can be moved at any time while they are in growth, provided that care is taken not to damage the roots too seriously in lifting the plant and that sufficient water is given to avoid the foliage and stems wilting. Lifting and moving plants in late autumn or winter is not a good idea, as the plants remain for many weeks with damaged roots, which are vulnerable to infection by fungi and bacteria found in the soil.

To plant or replant a delphinium root, dig out a large hole and fork a good handful of general fertilizer into the bottom. Position the plant in the hole and spread the roots out as far as possible. Fill up the hole with loose soil, at the same time lifting any fibrous roots and working the soil in among them. Tread down the soil around the plant to firm it, but take care not to create a water-logged sump by excessive pressure if the soil is heavy or wet. When moving plants in growth, it is advisable to water after planting and to reduce the rate of water loss from the foliage by fixing some shade netting around them.

FEEDING

While newly planted delphiniums should have been given enough nutrients to last through their first season, the food supplies for established plants that have been overwintered need to be replenished in late winter or early spring. Sprinkle two or three large handfuls (about a teacupful) of blood, fish and bonemeal or similar general fertilizer on the soil around each plant and lightly fork it into the surface. At the same time, sprinkle slug pellets among the plants to control the population of slugs and snails before they can attack the newly emerging shoots. No further fertilizer will be required during the season, unless the aim is to produce monster blooms for a flower show, when some additional feeding with high-nitrogen liquid feeds can boost early growth.

WATERING AND MULCHING

Water is as important for the growth of delphiniums as nutrients, but in dry weather it is not easy to supply this effectively from a can or hosepipe. It is better to minimize the amount of watering necessary by applying a thick mulch in late spring. Spent mush-

A vigorous plant before (left) and after (right) thinning, leaving five strong stems which will give better blooms

room compost is excellent for this purpose and efficiently smothers weed growth among the plants, whereas a mulch of well rotted farmyard manure can produce just the opposite effect. Watering may still be needed in hot weather and, until there are open flowers, it is probably best to apply this from an overhead sprinkler. The water then runs off the foliage to the roots at the perimeter of the plant, rather than soaking the crown, which could significantly increase the chance of rot in the base of the plant.

THINNING

Many delphinium cultivars are naturally prolific in flowering shoots and the quality of bloom declines if all are allowed to grow. It is therefore worth thinning the shoots of the large-flowered perennials in early spring, so that the energies of the plant are concentrated on producing from five to about ten good blooms instead of 50 poor ones. A preliminary thinning can be done when the stems are just a few inches long and the surplus shoots provide ideal material for cuttings if they are detached carefully (see p. 38). The main thinning should be done when the stems are 1 ft (30 cm) or more long, so that malformed stems can be clearly seen. For a plant with many shoots, first cut out all flattened or otherwise distorted stems. Check the remainder for any signs of damage and select the most vigorous five or more as the ones to retain. Remove the surplus shoots by cutting them off at ground level. The number of stems to leave depends on the vigour of the plant and can vary from just two or three for a newly planted root or second year seedling, to ten or more for vigorous old plants in a herbaceous border. After thinning, the plants can look a very sorry sight, but they soon recover and stems thicken up and grow with renewed vigour.

23

STAKING

Delphinium flower stems are seldom very durable in bad weather and this is especially true at the time of thinning, when the stems are soft and easily snapped by the wind or even a late snowfall. To avoid such damage, put in a few small canes around each plant and tie a single strand of string from cane to cane to prevent the stems from being broken. Longer canes or twiggy sticks can be inserted later for the mature stems and the blooms. A few twiggy sticks usually provide all the support required by larkspurs and both the dwarf and branching types of delphiniums. Taking a little time over this job is very well worthwhile, for there is nothing worse then finding the plants wrecked by wind and rain at flowering time.

The best way to stake delphiniums is a matter for debate, as canes extending above the foliage are certainly obtrusive. One approach is to put in three or four canes per plant, with the top tie

Perennial delphiniums should be staked early in their growth; twine tied from cane to cane supports the stems

Left: inadequate support meant a broken bloom, even in the case of this Pacific Dwarf
Right: a top tie of thin twine stops the blooms of 'Summerfield Miranda' swinging out too far

around the plant hidden by the leaves at the base of the bloom spikes. With many delphinium cultivars, as long as the stems are not tied individually to the canes but are free to sway within the confines of the top tie, they should have sufficient strength to withstand quite bad weather. However, even with dwarfs like the Blue Fountains selection, the tiny blooms can break off when they are heavy with rain. Such damage can be avoided almost completely by using taller canes and adding a further ring of thin twine near the top of the bloom spikes, so that they are unable to swing far from the vertical. If carefully done, the ties need not be too unsightly and they seem a small price to pay for avoiding the misery created by broken-down plants (see figure 2, p. 26).

When inserting stakes or tying string around the plants, it is useful to look for signs of pests or diseases, such as damage from caterpillars or patches of mildew. The plants can then be sprayed before any problems get out of control (see p. 48). Putting on the top ties provides an ideal opportunity to admire the beauty of the flowers and to assess the quality of seedlings.

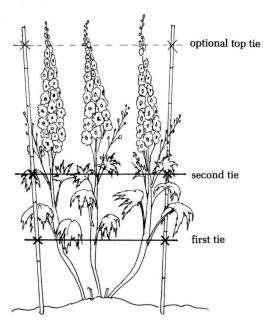

optional top tie

second tie

first tie

Figure 2: staking a plant using three or four canes and a few twine ties, added at the levels shown as the stems grow

AFTER FLOWERING

When the main flower spikes fade, the display is continued by side spikes or laterals. If these have flimsy stems, they should be tied in to the base of the main flowering stem, so that they do not flop down when wet with rain. Otherwise, the main bloom spike should be cut off at the base of the flower, unless one wishes to collect seed (see p. 28). As the flowers on the laterals fade, the flowering portion of these too should be cut off. The ties and support canes can then be removed and the stems of the plant drawn together, tied to a short cane and allowed to die down naturally.

After flowering, many delphiniums produce new shoots from the base that will give a second crop of flowers in the autumn. The production of these shoots can be stimulated by cutting off the first batch of stems at ground level as soon as the flowers fade. For good second blooms, it is important to thin out and support the stems, to give the plant some additional high-nitrogen fertilizer and to provide water as required. Caterpillars and mildew are often more of a problem than with the first flowers and it is worth spraying the plants to avoid damage.

In autumn, when the flower stems have withered and died down, the top growth should be cut off at an inch or two above ground level. All leaf debris and weeds should be cleared away from the base of the plants, as such material encourages and harbours slugs and snails, which can damage the crown buds during the dormant period. Spreading some coarse sand over the crowns may help deter slugs and snails, but it is not necessary to cover the plants in any other way as they are completely hardy and need no protection against frost. It is useful to check on the state of the plants by pulling lightly on the ends of the stems after cutting them down. If any stems pull out of the ground and show extensive rotting at the base, the plant will probably not survive the winter and plans should be made to replace it. When a plant has decayed, dig out the remnants and replace it in the spring with fresh stock from seedlings or cuttings raised the previous year.

After flowering, cut the seed heads off at the base of the bloom and leave the stems to die down; new growth at the base may yield another crop of flowers

Growing from seed

Starting from seed is the most economical way to obtain good delphiniums and is not difficult for most cultivated types. For species delphiniums, it is usually the only source of plants but, in this case, germinating the seeds and raising the plants poses many problems to tax the grower's skill.

OBTAINING SEED

The first task is to acquire viable seed. Most seed suppliers market selections of larkspurs, perennial garden hybrids and one or two species like *D. grandiflorum* and *D. cardinale*. The problem with these is that the quality of the plants they yield is rather low and the grower is faced with sorting the wheat from the chaff or being satisfied with second best. For top quality, seed should be purchased from delphinium specialists (see p. 63). Seed of species delphiniums is particularly difficult to find and anyone interested in the species should join a specialist plant society (see p. 63). Increasing interest in wild plants is leading to the emergence of seed suppliers with lists including delphiniums, particularly in the United States, and they can be located through various "plant finder" guides.

Seed can be saved, of course, from any delphinium already in the garden, although plants raised from this are often less good than the parents (see p. 57). Collect the seed when ripe and let it dry for a few days before packeting it for storage.

STORAGE

Once obtained, delphinium seed needs proper storage, since its viability declines quite rapidly at the temperature and humidity levels commonly found in our homes. This deterioration can be largely avoided by storing all delphinium seed in sealed containers, kept in the vegetable crisper compartment at the bottom of a domestic refrigerator. Delphinium seed is poisonous, so it is very important to ensure that the container is clearly labelled. It should certainly not be stored in a fridge if small children might have access.

Opposite: 'Blue Springs' is one of several dwarf seed selections

WHEN TO SOW

Seed can be sown and germinated at almost any time of year, but sowing in autumn and winter is not advisable without special facilities. Seeds of most garden types naturally germinate best at low soil temperatures. Indeed, newly germinated, self-sown seedlings can often be found emerging from the soil during mild spells in midwinter, although this could also be an indication that the seed requires a cold, wet soak before it will germinate. These features of the germination process reflect the alpine origin of most garden delphiniums and emphasize the fact that we should take account of the natural environment in which the plants grow when trying to raise species delphiniums from seed.

Perennial garden hybrid delphiniums can be raised from seed sown direct into the open ground from May to August, but losses through slugs, snails and other pests can be very high. It is preferable to raise the seedlings in pots or seed trays, as for most bedding plants. These can be sown in summer, but small seedlings must still be protected from attack by slugs and snails throughout the winter. Sowing in early spring avoids these problems and yields plants that can be brought into flower in late summer.

SOWING METHODS

Sow the seeds thinly on the surface of moist seed compost in small pots or seed trays. Add a little more compost so that the seeds are just covered over and lightly firm the surface. Use clean pots or trays and sterile compost, either loam-based or soilless, to

Seeds can be germinated on wet paper towel and transferred to individual pots when the roots appear

minimize the risk of disease. To ensure that the compost is sufficiently moist, stand the pots for a few minutes in a saucer or dish of shallow water, so that water rises up through the compost by capillary action. A few drops of liquid copper fungicide can be added to this water to reduce the risk of damping off. Cover the pot with a lid or aluminium foil to prevent the compost drying out and place it in a room where the temperature remains constant at near 60°F (15°C).

An alternative method, which is particularly valuable for species delphiniums or when very few seeds are available, is to germinate the seeds before they are planted in compost, by a process known as chitting. The seeds are spread on wet paper towel in a plastic container, which is then covered with a lid and kept in a warm room at about 60°F (15°C). As soon as any seed is found to have germinated, it should be removed with tweezers and planted in an individual 2-in. (5 cm) pot of moist seed compost. This approach also provides a clean and easy way of dealing with difficult seeds (such as *D. nelsoni*) that have to be kept in the fridge for a cold, wet soak for a period before they can be induced to germinate freely.

GERMINATION AND DEVELOPMENT OF SEEDLINGS

Germination times for delphinium seeds can vary from two or three days to several months. For garden hybrid perennials, the germination time ranges from five days for root emergence from very fresh seed, to upwards of three weeks from seed of slow-germinating cultivars, which include many of the dark blue ones. In seed mixtures, germination usually peaks at about 14 days, but can continue sporadically for several more weeks. This wide spread in germination times means that it is important to keep up the moisture level in the surface layer of compost for a substantial period after the first seedlings appear, otherwise germination of the remainder will be inhibited. Therefore, when seeds are germinated indoors in a warm room, it is necessary to keep the trays and pots covered. It is essential, however, for the seedlings to be placed in good light as soon as they start to come up in significant numbers. These partly conflicting requirements can be met by placing the seed pots under the transparent propagator tops for seed trays that are now widely available, allowing as much ventilation as possible. Good light is important to ensure sturdy growth of the seedlings, but strong direct sunshine through a window can "fry" young seedlings in a few minutes and some net shading should be provided if seedlings are kept on a sunny window ledge or a high shelf in the greenhouse.

Left: seedlings germinating 14 days after sowing; 40 seeds were sown in a 4-in. (10 cm) pot
Right: pots of seedlings covered with transparent tops

After seven to ten days, seedlings begin to develop the first true leaves. For most delphinium species and hybrids, these emerge from the point where the stem divides to form the stalks of the seed leaves or cotyledons but, in a few species, notably the dwarf red D. nudicaule, the first true leaves develop from a point below the surface of the compost. Further leaves develop and expand quite rapidly and, after four weeks, the seedlings should be ready to be pricked off into individual pots or spaced out in deep trays of potting compost. After pricking out, seedlings can be grown on for two to three weeks on the bench in a cool greenhouse, but they should be hardened off and moved outside as soon as possible. Seedlings from sowings in February and early March should be filling their pots with roots and will be ready for planting in the open ground from mid-May onwards.

Pricking out the seedlings of species delphiniums must always be done carefully, as many of them resent root disturbance and may go dormant. This can happen with both D. zalil and D. cardinale, which have tuberous roots, and with these it is advantageous to chit the seed, so that the germinated seeds can be planted in individual pots (see p. 31). Mixing pirimiphos-methyl dust with the compost reduces the risk of the seedling roots being eaten by the larvae of fungus flies (sciarids).

PLANTING OUT

Spring-sown seedlings of most garden delphiniums should flower well in the first year in late summer, provided they are kept in vigorous growth. They should be planted in fertile soil and

Left: seedlings pricked out into individual pots
Right: seedlings in 4-in. (10 cm) pots, hardened off and ready for
planting out in May

watered in dry spells. The soil should be prepared well before planting time in the same way as for mature plants (see p. 21). The ground used can be a display bed, the edge of a border for dwarf types, or a nursery bed in the vegetable garden for large-flowered perennials.

Seedlings of the large-flowered kinds can be planted close together in their first year, for only a single flower stem is normally produced. They may be planted as close as 10 in. (25 cm) apart in double row blocks, with 20 in. (50 cm) between the rows and paths about 3 ft (1 m) wide between the blocks to allow for cultivation, staking and tying of the blooms. It is worth forking a spoonful of dried blood into each planting hole to boost the initial growth of the seedlings. Where wireworm is a problem, it is advisable also to sprinkle some soil pesticide in the holes and on the surrounding soil, or there can be severe losses of seedlings. It is always necessary to protect newly planted seedlings against attack by slugs and snails, sprinkling slug pellets among the plants and spreading some sharp sand on the soil surface around each plant as an additional deterrent.

Seedlings in pots or boxes should be thoroughly watered just before planting out and, if the weather is hot and dry, the ground should be given a good soaking with a sprinkler the day before. No further watering should be required for several days after planting but, in hot spells or when there is a drying wind, it is worth checking daily and watering any seedlings that look to have dried out. The need for watering can be reduced by putting on a mulch, for example of mushroom compost, soon after the seedlings have been planted out.

Left: sturdy young seedlings used as bedding plants, seen here in early July before the flower stems grow

Right: the first blooms of young seedlings planted in rows

FLOWERING

Seedlings should grow rapidly during May and June, with considerable leaf expansion and stem thickening. Extension of the flower stem starts in July and some plants may be in flower by early August in good weather, although flowering from mid-August onwards is more common. A proportion of most batches of seedlings fails to flower the first season, but instead develops into squat plants with thick stems. Some seedlings also flower prematurely, with just a few florets on a wispy stem, rather than producing a flower stalk of usual size with a good large bloom. Such growths are probably best pinched off unless one is impatient to see the flower. Normal blooms are heavy when wet and seedlings should be supported with stakes and ties as for mature plants (see p. 24). Gales in August and September can otherwise cause havoc, uprooting plants and snapping the stems at ground level, with severe damage to the crown of the plant.

SELECTING PLANTS

The flower display in late summer from spring-sown seedlings can be just as spectacular as that of midsummer, but with seedlings one should take the chance to look at the flower critically and select the plants that are worth keeping.

To recognize the difference between good and bad seedlings, it is necessary to start with a clear idea of the features of good delphiniums, such as the named cultivars. Decide which of their characteristics you like most and then examine each seedling to see how it compares with your ideal. Look first at the individual florets and count the petals. Good seedlings should have at least 13 well formed petals, although whether they should be perfectly flat, rounded or with frilled edges is a matter of personal preference, as is their colour. The eye petals should form a neat cluster hiding the anthers and matching or contrasting with the colour of the outer petals, so that the floret makes a pretty individual flower.

Look next at the bloom spike as a whole and check that the size and number of individual florets and the length of spike are in proportion to the height of the plant. Very large florets on a tiny plant or a short bloom spike on a 6 ft (2 m) giant seem out of place. Overcrowding or irregular packing of the florets and gaps between them also spoil the general appearance of the blooms and should be regarded as faults. Another fault would be for the bloom to be shedding petals from the bottom florets before the top florets start to open. A good delphinium also needs a tough stem to support the flower in bad weather. Test the stem by lightly squeezing it between finger and thumb and reject seedlings with stems that seem soft. Working in this way, it is possible to select plants that will give fine displays of quality flowers in subsequent years.

Assessing the flowers: (left) poorly formed, almost single florets with just 5 or 6 petals on a seedling that should be discarded; (centre) nicely formed, well packed florets with good colour and neat eye on a seedling worth retaining; (right) beautiful florets with 13 petals of good form and a neat contrasting eye on a seedling from a cross between 'Emily Hawkins' and 'Icecap'

AFTER FLOWERING

When the blooms are finished, they should be cut off at the base of the flower and the plants allowed to die down. First year seedlings can normally be cut down in late November or December and all rubbish cleared away from the plot. This annual clear-up provides an opportunity to go round distributing slug pellets between the plants, so that their precious crown buds are protected from attack during the period of winter dormancy. Once the winter is past and new growth has started again in spring, last season's selected seedlings will have become this year's young mature plants and will need the same attention as other delphiniums already in the garden.

'Fenella' is a dependable plant in stunning blue, flowering in the middle of the season

Propagation

Most hybrid garden delphiniums, including named cultivars, do not breed true from seed and must be propagated vegetatively, either by dividing a mature plant into segments or by taking cuttings. Propagation from cuttings generates plants with a completely new root system and is the best way to keep the plant stock healthy. It is also the most convenient method of maintaining a good-quality stock of named cultivars, since it is easy to take one or two cuttings from the best plant of each cultivar without seriously disturbing the roots. Old plants showing signs of deterioration can then be replaced.

DIVISION

Increasing the stock of a favourite delphinium by division should be done in spring when the plant has started into growth. Dig around the plant to loosen the soil in the root area and then lift it out of the ground. It is wise to proceed cautiously as mature plants can be extremely heavy. If the plant has partially decayed in the centre, it may fall to pieces on lifting. However, this should not happen with healthy, vigorous plants, which can be divided by placing a pair of border forks back to back through the centre and levering the sections apart. If the remaining sections are large, they can be subdivided in the same way. Examine the pieces carefully, making sure that each has good roots and some shoots or crown buds. Use a sharp, sterile knife to cut away any obviously rotten sections of the old crown that remain attached to the division. Replanted in fresh soil, the divided plants quickly make new roots, but in sunny weather it is worth fixing some shading around them, so that the stems and leaves do not wilt. Provided the plants re-establish satisfactorily, they can be allowed to flower normally, although it is advisable to cut out any weak stems.

CUTTINGS

The techniques for taking and rooting cuttings of delphiniums are similar to those required for some other hardy perennials, such as lupins, but differ considerably from the procedures used with chrysanthemums or geraniums. The best material for cuttings is the young growth sprouting from the crown of the plant in early spring, when the shoots are 2–6 in. (5–15 cm) long. These shoots must be detached from the crown of the old plant, either by making a cut exactly at their junction with the crown, or by cutting into the woody crown tissue. It is usually necessary to clear away protective sand or soil to expose the points where the cuts are to be made. If a large number of cuttings is wanted, it is preferable to lift the plant from the soil and to work on a bench in more comfortable conditions.

The point where the cut should be made to detach a shoot is usually recognizable as a well defined constriction or "waist" right at the base of a stem. Starting from this point, a typical shoot has about $\frac{1}{4}$–$\frac{1}{2}$ in. (5–15 mm) of basal tissue with a brownish skin, leading into a section with many white or green leafless scales, from which the smooth stem with developing leaves emerges. Quite often, the point of attachment is on the underside of an almost horizontal old stem and can be very difficult to get at without digging up the plant. However, it is often advantageous to go for shoots emerging well down the crown, which are less likely to be spoiled by rot in the base than shoots emerging from the top of the crown. The latter are usually the first to suffer from rots associated with water lying in the hollow bases of old flower stems.

The reason for severing the shoot at its junction with the woody crown is to ensure that the cutting has the basal tissue attached,

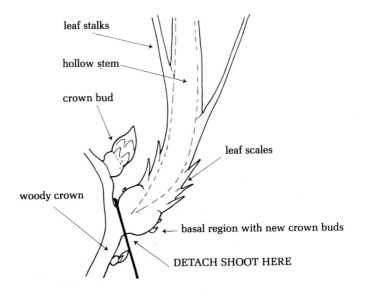

Figure 3: cross-section through a delphinium crown, showing typical features and the correct point at which to make the cut

Left: young growth in early spring provides ideal material for cuttings
Right: a root lifted and washed to show the points of attachment of
shoots to the crown at which cuts are made

this being the only material that will readily produce further basal
shoots. Unless new crown buds form, a rooted stem will simply
flower and die like a larkspur. It is often recommended that the
cut should be made in such a way as to obtain a shoot with a solid
base. This is certainly a desirable feature of a good cutting, as rot
organisms can develop inside a hollow stem, but it is not essential.
Roots are formed within the wall of the stem and new roots
emerge in a ring at the outer edge of the base of the cutting, not
from the central part. Cuttings with hollow bases root and behave
normally, so long as they have the section of basal tissue that will
produce the crown of the new plant.

Use a sharp knife or scalpel blade to detach the shoot by making
a clean cut. Sterilize the blade before each cut by wiping or
immersing it in a sterilant solution, in order to minimize the risk
of transmitting disease from plant to plant. If working in the
garden in sunny weather, store the cuttings in a labelled plastic
bag to avoid wilting.

It is worth cleaning up and trimming the cuttings before inserting them in the rooting medium, as they may be contaminated
with disease organisms present in the soil. This can be done easily
by holding the cuttings under a running tap to wash soil off the
base of the shoots and by using a soft $\frac{1}{2}$ in. (10 mm) paint brush to
dislodge material from crevices, taking care not to damage any
tiny crown buds. Use a sharp, clean blade to trim away damaged
tissue or old crown wood so that the base of the cutting is clean.

The essential requirements for rooting are that the cuttings are

39

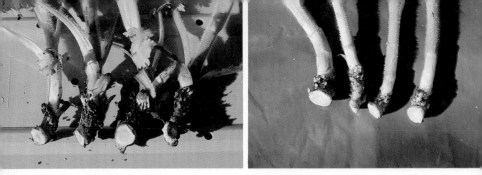

Cuttings before (left) and after (right) washing and trimming, with miniature crown buds already present

kept in good light and take up water. Delphiniums root best at low temperatures and it is unwise to use heated propagators, which often lead to rotting rather than rooting.

The simplest and one of the most reliable methods of rooting cuttings is to stand them in a jar of water, with a label to indicate the cultivar. Wash the cuttings free of any soil and pour tap water into the jar to a depth of 1–1½ in (25–40 mm). Do not use rainwater or add nutrients, for both can encourage algae. The cuttings can be dipped in a rooting hormone before inserting them in the jar, four or five to a 1 lb (0.5 kg) jam jar. Place the jar in good light on a sunny window ledge or on a high shelf in the greenhouse and check the water level daily. If a cutting fails to take up water and wilts, remove it and cut a thin slice off the base to re-open blocked capillaries in the stem. Soft cuttings with large leaves may wilt for a day or two and are best left in a shady position, or a large plastic bag can be placed over the cuttings jar. Remove any cutting that starts to rot and replace the remainder in clean water after washing off any slime that may have developed on the stems.

Using the water method, the process of root development can be seen and individual cuttings can be removed and potted up when the "brush" of roots reaches ½–1 in. (20–30 mm) long. Rooting is dependent on light and in February to March may take five weeks, while in April to May only three weeks or less is required.

A modification of the water method is to root the cuttings in a soil-free sterile medium, such as perlite or vermiculite. Clean cuttings should be dipped in rooting hormone and inserted about 1 in. (25 mm) deep in a bed of clean perlite or vermiculite in a dwarf pot or seed tray. Lightly firm the perlite around the cutting and pour a little water down the stem to ensure that it is held firmly and establishes capillary contact with the rooting medium. The pots and trays should then be stood in saucers or shallow trays of water that are topped up daily. Water rises up through the bed of perlite by capillary action and keeps the base of the cuttings moist, while the porous nature of the rooting medium allows air to circulate around the stem. Root development often seems more vigorous and uniform than with the water method. There also appears to be less danger that one rotting cutting will spread the infection to another in a batch.

The stage of root development for cuttings in perlite can be guessed from the appearance of the top growth. Immediately new roots start to form, the shoot begins to grow out, but it is wise to leave the cutting a week or more before removing it. The emergence of roots through the drainage holes of the pot is perhaps the best indicator that there is sufficient root to justify taking out some of the cuttings for potting up. Any cuttings with too little root can be replaced in the perlite, providing they show no signs of rotting of the basal tissue.

Freshly rooted delphinium cuttings should be potted up individually in $3\frac{1}{2}$ or 4 in. (9 or 10 cm) pots, using any good potting compost of either John Innes or soilless type. Partly fill the pot with moist compost and place the cutting so that the base is at the centre with the roots spreading out radially. Cuttings from perlite should be planted without disturbing the perlite granules that adhere to the roots. Insert a split cane alongside the stem at this stage, when it can be positioned without damaging the base of the

Left: rooting cuttings by the water method, with a little washed gravel at the bottom of the jar
Right: rooting cuttings in moist perlite

Left: cuttings rooted in perlite quickly make extensive root systems
Right: a pinched-out cutting with new growth from the base, ready for planting out

cutting. Add compost around the roots so that the base of the cutting is about 1 in. (25 mm) below the surface. Consolidate the compost around the stem by gently tapping the pot on the bench, since this is less likely to damage the fragile roots than firming the compost with one's fingers. Tie the stem to the split cane and pinch out the growing point with thumb and forefinger, to encourage new growth from the base. Lightly water the cutting from the top to establish good capillary contact between the roots and the compost and leave the pot in a cool spot for a day or two. Once the cuttings have recovered, they grow quickly and should be hardened off ready for planting in the open ground in their flowering positions as soon as the pot is full of roots. Production of a new plant is complete as soon as new shoots emerge from the compost at the base of the stem.

Delphinium cuttings can be rooted in many other ways, for example by inserting them in the soil alongside the parent plants or in a bed of clean sand in a cold frame. Such methods can be quite successful as long as good cuttings are used, but rooting is very dependent on weather conditions and losses can be high.

Hybridization

One of the great joys of gardening is to see plants that you have grown from tiny seeds come into flower, and that pleasure increases if you have obtained the seeds by pollinating the flowers of the seed parent by hand. This is quite easy to do with delphiniums and the resulting seedlings can be seen in flower the following season, which makes them ideal plants to work with for anyone interested in trying to breed their own plants.

CHOOSING THE PARENTS

The first step is to choose the cultivars to use as parents. For the seed parent, choose a plant that readily sets lots of seed. Some well known cultivars, such as 'Mighty Atom' and 'Bruce', and all the creamy yellow cultivars usually set little seed and should be avoided. Other cultivars, like 'Sandpiper', have stigmas that are easily damaged or are difficult to pollinate owing to the presence of leaflets growing out of the centre of the flower. These are better used as pollen parents. There are also cultivars that make poor pollen parents because they produce very little pollen.

While the practicalities of achieving successful pollination must be taken into consideration in choosing the parents for a cross, it is even more important to use only plants that regularly produce top-quality flowers. Experience soon teaches the hard lesson that most of the desirable qualities of garden delphiniums are genetically recessive, which means that all the seedlings raised from a cross between a good plant and a poor-quality one are likely to be poor. Growing such seedlings is a waste of time and garden space. Crosses between good cultivars, however, usually yield a sufficiently high proportion of interesting seedlings to make growing 20 to 30 seedlings very rewarding. Good examples are the crosses: 'Olive Poppleton' (white, seed parent) × 'Cream Cracker' (cream, pollen parent); 'Emily Hawkins' (pale violet) × 'Cassius' (dark blue-mauve); and 'Royal Flush' (dusky pink) × 'Rosemary Brock' (dusky pink). All these yield seedlings of fine quality in interesting colours (see p. 44).

Parents for a cross can be chosen to obtain flowers of a particular colour, bloom spikes of a particular form, dwarf growth or whatever characteristic takes one's fancy. However, the prediction of the outcome of any cross requires a great deal of

A high-quality seedling from a cross between the pale violet 'Emily Hawkins' and dark blue-mauve 'Cassius'

information about the parents and, for most growers, it is sufficient to leave the results to chance. Delphiniums are such complicated hybrids that the information is often not available anyway. Anyone interested in more detailed consideration of the inheritance of colour and other characters of delphiniums should consult the Year Books published by the Delphinium Society.

44

MAKING THE CROSS

To make a cross, the flowers of the seed parent must be "prepared" by removing the anthers before they shed any pollen, which could cause self-fertilization. This is best done just as the floret is about to open. Some hybridists prise open the bud to remove the anthers, leaving the petals intact. In order to avoid all risk of unwanted pollination, it seems sensible to remove the petals too, since their purpose is to attract pollinating insects. Pulling the petals off the flower bud exposes the cluster of eye petals surrounding the anthers and undeveloped ovaries. The eye petals and the spur should then be carefully pulled off and the anthers can be removed by gently gripping them between finger and thumb and pulling them off. This must be done carefully as rough handling can easily damage the stigmas. The stigmas are usually not clearly visible yet and a further three or four days may be required for them to develop and become receptive to pollen. As the exposed seed pods and stigmas sometimes fail to develop, particularly if the weather is very hot or wet, it is always advisable to prepare several florets for pollination.

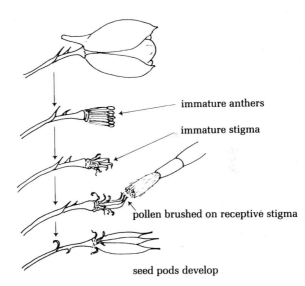

immature anthers

immature stigma

pollen brushed on receptive stigma

seed pods develop

Figure 4: to hand-pollinate a delphinium floret, remove the sepals and eye petals from an opening bud and then pinch off the immature anthers to leave just the immature stigmas; after two or three days, dust pollen from another delphinium on the tips of the receptive stigmas

Above (left): stages in stripping petals and eye petals and removing anthers, with buds ready for stripping at the top and stripped florets at the bottom; (right) florets with stigmas ready for pollination

Below (left): a good crop of hand-pollinated seed maturing; (right) these pretty white flowers were obtained by making a cross between two whites to guarantee white seedlings

The undeveloped stigmas initially curve downwards but, as they mature, they extend in length and turn upwards with a sticky receptive prong at the tip. At this stage, pollination can be carried out, either by dusting pollen on the tip of each stigma from a pollen-loaded brush (a small artist's camel-hair paint brush is suitable), or by bringing pollen-loaded anthers from flowers of the other parent into contact with the tip of the stigmas. Since one cannot tell immediately if pollination has been successful, it is worth repeating the operation the following day. Mark the pollinated florets with a label. If pollination has been successful, the seed pods start to swell up and then require a few weeks to mature and ripen. Seed set may be poor in wet weather, if the pollen is washed off by rain, and in very hot weather, when the stigmas remain receptive for only a short time.

RIPENING AND HARVESTING

When small numbers of florets have been hand-pollinated, it is practicable to protect the seed pods against caterpillar and bird attack. A small piece of nylon stocking can be wrapped around the cluster of pods from each floret and tied both around the floret stalk and beyond the end of the seed pods. The disadvantage of doing this is that it is less easy to check on ripening and it is also necessary to make sure that earwigs do not creep inside and defeat all the precautions. In order not to lose any precious seeds, the seed pods should be harvested just before they would split open naturally. The ripening of seeds on adjacent florets gives a good idea when this should be done. Take the harvested pods indoors, lay them on clean paper in a box and allow them to dry and split open naturally before separating out the seeds. Fresh seed germinates well and it is sensible to sow some of the seeds immediately. However, seed that is to be stored should be allowed to dry for a few more days and should then be packeted, labelled and stored in a sealed dry container in the refrigerator, where it can safely remain until the following spring.

Pests and diseases

Delphiniums are not usually subject to severe pest or disease problems during the normal flowering season, although precautions must always be taken to avoid damage by slugs and snails. The simplest way to avoid the build up of disease is to keep a watchful eye on the plants as they grow and to take action to check any outbreaks before these get out of control.

SLUGS AND SNAILS

During the period of winter dormancy and in early spring, crown buds and newly emerging shoots may suffer unseen damage from slugs and caterpillars living beneath the soil surface. It is possible to control slug populations by regular applications of pellets or other proprietary slug killers, but it is equally important to clear away fallen leaves, weeds and other decaying vegetation that attract and harbour slugs and small snails. Covering the crowns with a mound of sharp sand or coarse ash is a further deterrent. Slug pellets based on methiocarb are more effective than preparations containing metaldehyde, but both should be used carefully as they are very poisonous to animals. Delphiniums are attractive to slugs and snails at all times of year and the young growth of newly planted seedlings, cuttings and container-grown plants all need protecting from them.

CATERPILLARS

The growing points of delphinium flower stems may be damaged at any stage by caterpillars of the delphinium moth (golden plusia). These usually occur singly and are first detectable on the young leaves at the top of a stem, when part of a leaf appears to be rolled up. Uncurling the leaf reveals that it is stuck together with silken webbing and, if present, the small green caterpillar with black spots can be eliminated. If these caterpillars are not destroyed, they rapidly migrate down into the growing point, where they eat the developing flower spike and leaves. Hand-picking is the best method of control in small gardens but, where large numbers of delphiniums are grown, all the plants should be sprayed thoroughly as soon as damage is seen, using an insecticide such as pirimiphos-methyl or permethrin.

Late blooms, especially those of seedlings and secondary growths flowering from July onwards, can be damaged by another caterpillar of the "looper" or "geometer" variety. This climbs the stems at night, bores a characteristic hole though the side of the flower buds and, once inside, eats out the anthers and stigmas before moving on to another bud. Control is difficult because the caterpillars are usually completely hidden and it is probably not worth attempting except where plants are grown for show blooms or when seed is required. Caterpillars, such as those of the angleshades moth, may also eat flower buds and immature seed pods. Seeds are taken by birds, particularly bullfinches, but in most seasons seed is more often spoiled by mildew or botrytis (grey mould).

DELPHINIUM LEAFMINER

The leaves of delphiniums may be affected by the delphinium leafminer. The adult flies puncture the young leaves when feeding and small whitish green spots develop on the foliage, but more

A flattened multiheaded stem caused by fasciation (see p. 50)

severe damage can be caused by the larvae, which live and feed in "blotch mines" inside the leaves. These mines are usually to be found on lower leaves, starting near the point of a leaf and spreading towards the stalk. The affected areas dry up and go brown, so that the lower leaves wither and die prematurely. Serious damage can be avoided by spraying with an insecticide such as pirimiphos-methyl, malathion or HCH, as soon as signs of leaf mining are seen.

FASCIATION

As the plant stems grow, distorted growth is sometimes seen, with the stem flattened and leaves irregularly positioned and mis-shapen. With further growth, the stem may divide or produce monstrous flower heads that curl up or split. Sometimes the flower spike has just a few buds and long bare sections with whiskers instead of flowers. All these are examples of a condition termed fasciation. This reflects irregularities in the process of cell division as the stem develops and it may have a variety of causes. Often it may result from checks to growth during spells of cold, frosty weather in early spring. Heavy manuring seems to increase the chance of fasciation and some cultivars are certainly more susceptible to such growth abnormalities than others. Fasciation, accompanied by a mass of aborted shoots at ground level, can also be caused by a soil bacterium, *Corynebacterium fascians*, which causes the disease known as leafy gall. This organism can be spread from plant to plant on the knife used in taking cuttings unless the blade is sterilized before each cut. Fasciation is not normally a cause for concern and it is usually sufficient to cut out distorted stems when the plants are thinned in early spring. Seedlings that are found to fasciate regularly should not be kept.

MILDEW

Mildew can be a serious problem, especially from late July onwards. This disease is easily recognized by the powdery white deposits that develop on the upper surface of leaves and on the flowers, and it can ruin the appearance of the plant. Claims were often made in the past that some strains of delphinium were immune to mildew, but that is certainly not the case today, although there are considerable variations in susceptibility between one cultivar and another. Development of mildew can be minimized by good cultivation, ensuring that the plants are not short of water at the root in dry weather, and growing them suffi-ciently far apart for free air circulation among the plants. It is advisable to protect plants against mildew by spraying with a systemic fungicide before the flower buds start to open. Fungicides based on bupirimate with triforine give good control. Mildew is carried over from year to year on growths and remnants of old stems at the base of the plants, so clearing away all rubbish from the base of the plants in autumn is good practice.

VIRUS DISEASES

Aphids do not colonize delphiniums as the plants are protected naturally by an "anti-feedant", but they do visit the plants and may transmit virus diseases to them. Viruses can also be transmitted by soil pests such as eelworms (nematodes). Garden delphiniums therefore frequently carry a variety of virus diseases, but this is not important unless a particular virus causes poor growth or obvious abnormalities of the flowers. Virus diseases in delphiniums have not been extensively studied in recent years and it is seldom possible to associate particular symptoms with specific viruses.

The most important precaution any gardener can take is to get to know the plants and the normal appearance of the flower so that changes are recognizable. Plants that suddenly develop variegated leaves with pale yellow stripes or unusual patterning of the leaf colouring should be suspect. Another indication of possible virus disease would be abnormal florets, for example florets that do not open properly and have no anthers but a multitude of stigmas, or florets with an unusually small number of twisted petals and streaky colour. Plants showing serious abnormalities of this sort must be replaced whenever possible and all material from diseased plants should be destroyed by burning. It should be remembered that tools used to cut down or dig out these plants can be contaminated and they should be disinfected before further use. It is also advisable to wash one's hands before handling any other plant. The site of the plants should not be replanted with another delphinium for a year or more, unless the old soil is removed and replaced.

A serious difficulty in recognizing virus disease symptoms is to distinguish them from changes resulting from natural mutations of the plant, but this is not something the average gardener needs to worry about. In practice, any change that leads to the loss of the good qualities of a delphinium should be a reason for removing the plant from the garden and replacing it with fresh stock. Most named cultivars go steadily downhill as a result of mutations and it is therefore important to propagate only from the best plants available. This is also a good argument for growing cultivars of recent origin, rather than cultivars of mainly historical interest.

ROTTING

The most troublesome disease of perennial delphiniums is rotting of the crown, which causes winter losses. Rotting occurs as the result of bacteria or fungi from the soil invading the tissues of the rootstock, but it is not well understood why this happens in some situations and not in others. The problem often seems to start where slugs have eaten crown buds or where an unsupported stem has broken off below ground level. It is certainly accentuated if the ground is waterlogged, or if the plant tissues are too soft because of excessive use of high-nitrogen fertilizers or manure. Some cultivars are also more susceptible to rotting than others. Another cause can be root damage from eelworms. When this is involved, rotting is not confined to the crown and blackened areas can be seen on the surface of the fibrous roots as well.

Unfortunately, there are no remedies for crown rot other than good cultivation, which should aim to produce well drained soil and hard growth. Any cultivars known to be particularly susceptible to rotting should be propagated regularly, so that mature plants can be replaced with young stock. Where a plant does die as the result of rot in the crown, it is advisable to dig out as much soil as possible and remove all root remnants. The site should then be replenished with clean soil before replanting. The build up of soil pathogens can be minimized by moving delphiniums around the garden, rather than growing them continuously on the same site for many years.

A selection of delphiniums to grow

The plants we grow in our gardens are often impulse-buys, gifts from friends or whatever is obtainable locally. For delphiniums, however, it is usually necessary to go to specialists to find plants or seeds of the highest quality and one may then have a long list to choose from. The following selection of delphiniums which are generally available is a personal one, with the emphasis on those species, seed selections and named cultivars that should delight the grower with their flowers. Heights are given in brackets.

'Rosemary Brock', a dusky pink with blooms and florets of particularly good form

NAMED CULTIVARS

The most widely grown delphiniums are the perennial hybrids and the named cultivars set the standards by which all others should be judged. Many of the cultivars available today are more than 20 years old, but some specialist nurseries also list recent introductions from amateur raisers. Plants are now normally sold as young rooted cuttings in early summer. Planted directly into the open ground, they quickly become fine specimens and will produce a bloom in the autumn, although a full display should not be expected until the next year. This short list includes only cultivars that make reliable perennial garden plants and illustrates the range of colours and heights available.

For a white delphinium, few cultivars are as attractive as '**Olive Poppleton**' (5½ ft/1.8 m), in which the pure white petals are set off by a honey-brown eye (see p. 19). Moderately tall, with broad, tapering blooms, this is one of the earliest delphiniums to flower and its first shoots sometimes suffer frost damage. '**Sandpiper**' (4½ ft/1.5 m) has the same problem, but the white florets with contrasting dark brown eye and the lovely shape of the blooms of this compact grower are worth the risk.

Cream florets with a yellow eye are very pretty and here there is little to choose between the two Blackmore & Langdon cultivars, '**Butterball**' (4 ft/1.2 m) and '**Sungleam**' (4½ ft/1.5 m). 'Sungleam' is a prolific producer of shoots and needs to be drastically thinned to obtain good blooms (see p. 56).

Also prolific in shoots is '**Rosemary Brock**' (5½ ft/1.8 m), having deep dusky pink florets with a dark brown eye and beautifully regular blooms (see p. 53). Similar colouring, but with a white eye to contrast with the petal colour, is provided by the solid blooms of '**Royal Flush**' (4½ ft/1.5 m) which, like the preceding, is late-flowering (see p. 56). For a paler colour, the pastel pink of '**Cherub**' (5 ft/1.7 m) is very attractive and the florets are of good form.

For flowers in a very pale, campanula-violet shade, '**Gillian Dallas**' (5 ft/1.7 m) makes an excellent border plant, with charming frilled florets, but must not be over-fed as the stems become very soft (see p. 56). '**Tiddles**' (5 ft/1.7 m) has similar colouring and interesting, fully double florets. '**Emily Hawkins**' (5½ft/1.8 m) flowers earlier than either of these and has pretty, pale violet florets with a light brown eye (see pp. 12 and 58).

Pale pastel blue overlaid with a pinkish tinge is the colour combination most likely to be found in a batch of mixed seedlings, but

Opposite: splendid blooms on a plant of 'Sandpiper', raised from a cutting rooted early the previous year

Above: three plants of 'Sungleam', grown from cuttings taken the previous year, produce a fine show in the Wisley delphinium trials

Below (left): 'Royal Flush', a reliable delphinium of medium height; (right): the pale shades of 'Gillian Dallas' combine well with other border plants

one seldom encounters seedlings that are as good as the old-timer, **'Fanfare'** (6 ft/2 m). This cultivar flowers early in the season and can produce very large, densely packed blooms.

One of the last cultivars to flower is **'Gordon Forsyth'** (6 ft/2m), which has flat florets of a pure amethyst colour with a small grey eye. The spikes are long and regular, but are often badly spoiled by mildew, so this cultivar should be sprayed with a systemic fungicide before the flowers open (see p. 59).

Most purple delphiniums also tend to be rather susceptible to mildew and should be given a precautionary fungicidal spray before flowering. The rich, velvety sheen of a purple such as **'Bruce'** (6 ft/2 m) then stays free from nasty white blotches and looks wonderful. The large blooms of this cultivar are ideal for exhibition. **'Cassius'** (5½ ft/1.8 m) is another late-flowerer, with broad tapering blooms that can have a purple tinge. The blooms look best, however, in seasons when the purple does not develop and the flowers are then a fine dark blue.

The traditional colour for delphiniums is blue and for this there is a range of cultivars differing in height and flowering season. For early flowers, the pale blue of **'Loch Leven'** (4½ ft/1.5 m) looks lovely near the front of a border (see p. 59) and, at the back, **'Cristella'** (6 ft/2 m) can be striking, for the white eye contrasts strongly with the mid-blue florets. **'Lock Nevis'** (6 ft/2.2 m), from the same raiser as 'Lock Leven', was for many years the finest blue for exhibition, but good stock is now difficult to obtain. Some mid-season cultivars are **'Fenella'** (5½ ft/1.8 m; see p. 36) or the very similar new introduction, **'Nicholas Woodfield'**, in deep gentian-blue with a black eye; **'Lord Butler'** (4½ ft/1.5 m), with very neat blooms in pure Cambridge blue that are ideal as cut flowers; and **'Tiny Tim'** (4 ft/1.2 m), which is very attractive with a ginger brown eye to light up the dark blue florets. For late flowers, the pale blue of **'Crown Jewel'** (6½ ft/2.2 m) is useful at the back of a border, but the heavy blooms are often gappy and need careful support.

SEED SELECTIONS

Seed saved from the best delphinium in the garden or given by friends may produce some good plants, but the results depend on the quality of other delphiniums in the neighbourhood that insect pollinators also visit. Seedlings of more reliable quality can be achieved by using seed obtained from specialists, which is saved from large collections of named cultivars or from carefully selected plants of their own raising. Such seed gives a mixture of colours and a range of sizes, but there should be few poor-quality

Left: the tall 'Gordon Forsyth' flowers towards the end of the normal delphinium season
Right: 'Loch Leven', an excellent short-growing delphinium

seedlings with single flowers. By comparison, most ordinary commercial packeted seed produces a high proportion of inferior plants, with poorly formed or single florets and irregular bloom spikes. Pacific Giants, in particular, now bear very little resemblance to the originals, except that they may still come fairly true to colour. More interesting are the '**New Century Hybrids/Dreaming Spires**' selection and the dwarf selections such as '**Blue Fountains**', '**Blue Heaven**' and the "Pacific dwarfs", '**Blue Springs**' (see p. 29). All dwarf selections yield many poor seedlings, but one can usually find some with flowers of reasonable quality on plants growing no more than 3 ft (1 m) tall.

BELLADONNAS

As with the large-flowered perennial hybrids, several named cultivars of these single-flowered branching types are available. Old favourites are violet-blue '**Lamartine**' (see p. 60) and the white '**Moerheimii**' (4 ft/1.2 m), both available from garden centres. A more recent cultivar in bright gentian-blue is '**Piccolo**', which is free-flowering and short-growing.

Opposite: 'Emily Hawkins', raised by the author, has gained a First Class Certificate in the Wisley trials

Belladonna delphiniums can also be raised from seed, which is available from most seedsmen for mixed colours and for the white **'Casablanca'** selection. **'Connecticut Yankees'** is another seed selection, giving a mixture of single-flowered blooms in shades of blue on short plants with a branching growth habit.

DWARF HYBRIDS

Several different seed selections of these charming dwarf delphiniums, hybrids of *D. grandiflorum* and *D. chinense*, are available and all should be treated as half-hardy annuals. If sown in February or early March, they flower well in August or September. **'Blue Mirror'** (12 in./30 cm) is a particularly pretty selection, with spurless, bright mid-blue florets facing upwards. An old selection, **'Blue Butterfly'**, is still obtainable and there are recent introductions, such as **'Blue Elf'** and **'Sky Blue'**. The latter opens almost pure white, slowly developing to a very pale blue with dark veining on the backs of the petals and is very attractive.

SPECIES DELPHINIUMS

The major seedsmen offer a few delphinium species and all are worth trying, as they provide unusual colours and an interesting contrast to the normal garden delphiniums.

'Lamartine' is a well known Belladonna

The dwarf 'Blue Mirror' is easily grown from seed for use in bedding

For the annual border, the '**Blue Cloud**' selection of D. *consolida* (20 in./50 cm) gives extensively branched plants with feathery foliage, which become covered with a mass of small, dark blue flowers with long spurs and provide a carpet of colour when planted in large groups.

A much taller plant for the perennial border is D. *denudatum* (4 ft/1.2 m), which can be easily raised from seed and flowered the first summer if sown early. It has a branching habit like a belladonna, but the small pale blue flowers are very widely spaced.

D. *cashmerianum* (10 in./25 cm) is a fascinating dwarf species for the rock garden or alpine house (see p. 62). It is often confused with other species such as D. *brunonianum* and the true plant may not be what is obtained, either when growing from seed or when plants are purchased, although they are all interesting. The violet-blue flowers with very short spurs are reminiscent of those of an aconitum. A good companion plant is D. *nudicaule* (10 in./25 cm), which has orange-red tubular flowers held above the rounded undissected leaves. Plants are easily raised from seed and will flower the first summer. The tuberous rootstocks are hardy and can survive for many years in a pot or a well drained site in the rock garden.

The most spectacular of the readily available species are both plants that, after flowering, require dry conditions to avoid

61

D. cashmerianum has unusual, almost hooded flowers

rotting of their tuberous rootstocks. It is therefore preferable to grow them to flower from seed in one year, but this is not easy since both the yellow-flowered *D. zalil* (3 ft/1 m) and the scarlet *D. cardinale* (4½ ft/1.5 m) are rather temperamental (see pp. 10 and 12). The interesting seeds of *D. zalil*, with rows of frilly scales, germinate easily and are best sown in individual pots of free-draining compost, so that they can grow on without the root disturbance caused by pricking out. Well grown plants produce large primary spikes and many long secondary spikes on wiry stems above feathery foliage. With care, *D. cardinale* can be flowered in summer from early sowings, but small seedlings also resent drying or disturbance of the roots and readily go dormant. If dormant roots are overwintered in pots in the greenhouse, they often start into new growth in January and the scarlet flowers are then produced over a long period in early summer.

Further information

BOOKS

Delphiniums, Ronald C. Parrett. Penguin Handbooks PH71, Penguin Books Ltd, 1961.
Delphiniums, Colin Edwards. J. M. Dent & Sons Ltd, 1981.
Delphiniums, The Complete Guide, Colin Edwards. Crowood Press, 1989.

GARDENS TO VISIT

Trials of delphiniums are grown at:
Wisley Garden, The Royal Horticultural Society, Wisley, Woking, Surrey GU23 6QB
Harlow Car Garden, The Northern Horticultural Society, Crag Lane, Harrogate, North Yorks HG3 1QB

The national collection of delphinium cultivars is maintained at:
Temple Newsam Park, Leeds, West Yorks LS15 0AD

SPECIALIST SOCIETIES

The Delphinium Society Mrs S. E. Bassett, "Takakkaw", Ice House Wood, Oxted, Surrey RH8 9DW
The Hardy Plant Society Mrs J. Sambrook, 214 Ruxley Lane, West Ewell, Surrey KT17 9EU
The Alpine Garden Society E. M. Upward, Lye End Link, St Johns, Woking, Surrey GU21 1SW

Seeds of cultivated and species delphiniums are available to members of the above societies.

SPECIALIST SUPPLIERS

The following supply named cultivars and seeds:
Blackmore & Langdon Ltd, Stanton Nurseries, Pensford, Bristol BS18 4JL
Butterfields Nursery, Harvest Hill, Upper Bourne End, Bucks SL8 5JJ
Rougham Hall Nurseries, Ipswich Road, Rougham, Bury St Edmunds, Suffolk IP30 9LZ

A lovely salmon-orange delphinium from the University Hybrids grown at Wisley Garden

Woodfield Brothers, 71 Townsend Road, Tiddington, Stratford-on-Avon, Warwicks CV37 7DF

Seeds of species delphiniums are available from:
Chiltern Seeds, Bortree Stile, Ulverston, Cumbria LA12 7PB
Thompson & Morgan, London Road, Ipswich, Suffolk IP2 0BA